WE ARE ALL AMERICANS

UNDERSTANDING DIVERSITY

FIVE PONDS PRESS

WACCABUC, NEW YORK

A NOTE TO TEACHERS AND STUDENTS

It is impossible to include every group that has made contributions to life in America, impossible to note every accomplishment, impossible to thank *all* the men, women, girls, and boys who worked so hard to make a better life for themselves and in doing so, made our country—and the world—a better place. I would need 10,000 books to do that! It is my sincere hope this book will inspire you to continue learning about all the wonderful people who make America unique, and to explore and celebrate your own special heritage.

—Joy Masoff

TABLE OF CONTENTS

THE AUTHOR GRATEFULLY ACKNOWLEDGES THE ENORMOUS CONTRIBUTION AND GUIDANCE OF:

Dr. Virginia Yans-McLaughlin, *Board of Governors Distinguished Service Professor of American History, Rutgers University*

Dr. Jose C Moya, *Professor of History, UCLA and Barnard College; Director: Barnard Forum on Migration*

FIVE PONDS PRESS ADVISORY GROUP:

Dr. Melissa Matusevich, *Assistant Professor of Curriculum and Instruction, East Carolina University; Former supervisor of Social Studies and Library Media, Montgomery County (VA) Public Schools*

Dr. Donald Zeigler, *Professor of Geography and Political Science, Old Dominion University, Norfolk (VA)*

REVIEWERS

SPECIAL THANKS FOR THE ENCOURAGEMENT AND CONTRIBUTIONS OF THE FOLLOWING EDUCATORS:

Brenda Randolph, *Africa Access*

Lara Samuels, *Hanover County (VA)*

Anita Parker, *Virginia Beach (VA)*

Denise Williams, *Virginia Beach (VA)*

Jason Deryck-Mahlke, *John Jay High School (NY)*

Kathy Morrison, *Retired Supervisor for Social Studies, K-12 Hanover County, (VA)*

Five Ponds Press books are available at a special discount when purchased in bulk for educational use. Contact Special Sales Dept. at Five Ponds Press or email info@fivepondspress.com

Copyright ©2006 by Joy Masoff
All rights reserved. Published by
Five Ponds Press, Waccabuc, NY 10597
Library of Congress Cataloging-in-Publication data available

ISBN 13: 978-0-9727156-2-1
ISBN 10: 0-9727156-2-2

First printing July 2006
10 9 8 7 6 5 4 3 2 1   Printed in the USA

*This 50-year-old poster
promised immigrants a better life.*

ALL CREATED EQUAL

Imagine if someone decided that everyone with blue eyes was a liar, or that all people with curly hair cheated. Would that be fair? What if someone told you that because you had freckles, you couldn't go to the movies? That would be awful!

Ever since the first contact between the American Indians and explorers from Europe, people in this country have sometimes judged others by where they came from and what they looked like, not by the kinds of people they were.

Can America become a land where all people are treated equally?

WHO ARE YOU?

"Where do you live? Where do you go to school?" These are questions someone might ask to get to know you better. "Where did your family come from?" The answer to *that* question may tell you a lot of really cool things about you and your friends.

ALL IN THE FAMILY

Maybe your grandparents came from Italy. Perhaps your parents came from Mexico. Maybe you were born in India. Americans have come from all over the world. Some families have just arrived, and some have been here for hundreds of years. Others have been here only a few **generations** (jen-er-A-shunz). Generations are a way to trace your family back in time by counting parents, grandparents, great-grandparents, and so on.

OLD AND NEW

No matter where you were born, you have something very special—a **culture**—the ways you eat, sing, dress, pray, dance, and celebrate. These great **traditions** came with your family when they first arrived in America.

These girls are dressed in the styles of their native lands. They are proud to share their traditions with one another.

When people with different cultural traditions share them, it makes life more fun. It happened as new arrivals brought things such as pizza and pop music, and it is still happening as people from other lands bring new ways of doing things.

WE ARE ALL ALIKE

Every year more than one million people move to America. Many are kids your age. They might speak in a way you find hard to understand. They might wear head-coverings all the time or love spicy food, but they are children who love to laugh, sing, and play...kids just like you.

AMERICAN SALAD

Imagine a big bowl. Throw in lettuce, carrots, and tomatoes. Toss in chicken and peppers. Now top it with a tasty dressing. The lettuce still looks like lettuce, but mixed with the other flavors, it tastes different. This colorful salad tastes great.

America is a lot like that. People from many different lands have brought their **customs**—the beliefs and habits of the places from which they came—and all of those things have been thrown into the same "bowl" and "tossed" together.

A BEAUTIFUL DREAM

Americans of all generations have had something very important in common— dreams of life, liberty, and the pursuit of happiness. This book will tell you about the long journey we have taken to make those dreams come true.

WHY DO WE NEED DIVERSITY?

Which set of pencils would be more fun to use? Diversity is a lot like a set of colored pencils— a mix of bright, bold, things!

What if you had to eat the same cereal at every meal all year long? What if music had only one note? What if there was only one TV station? Life would be so dull!

Diversity (de-ver-suh-tee) adds excitement to our lives. But what exactly is diversity? It's a collection of different things, ideas, or people. As folks came to America from different lands, they brought diverse ways of doing things.

Because of diversity, we have all sorts of amazing things such as new kinds of music to listen to and yummy things to eat!

HOW DOES DIVERSITY HAPPEN?

Long ago, people rarely left home. The towns where they were born were the places they died. There were no ships, trains, or airplanes to move them so they never saw people who looked different.

For thousands of years, on every continent, as cultures met for the first time, people reacted with surprise...and sometimes fear. They did not understand that we are really all the same.

THE HALF-HORSE MAN?

In 1493 a German mapmaker drew one of the first maps of the Americas. He added drawings based on stories written by ancient explorers that described what they *thought* they had seen on their travels to new places.

People looked at the drawings on the map and wondered, "Are the peoples of the New World a strange race of monsters? Do the men really have six arms?"

Think about this: If you had never seen a horse and then saw a man sitting on one, you *might* think he was part man, part animal.

If you had never seen someone with really long, blonde hair curling down her back, you *might* think she was covered with yellow fur.

The man who drew these pictures had heard stories about strange people in faraway places, but the truth is, there *are* no people with six arms or yellow furry skin. We are much more alike than the first explorers believed.

I'M SCARED!

As people from different places began to meet, they were surprised by what they saw. The discovery of people who looked *sort of* like them, but not quite the same, was often a big shock!

Here is a typical reaction. A young Nigerian boy who was taken as a slave from Africa in the 1700s wrote these words about the first Europeans he saw: *"I asked if we were about to be eaten by those white men with horrible looks, red faces and long hair."*

Jamestown, Virginia was one of the first places where American Indians and Europeans lived side by side. Do you think they got along?

A DIVERSE NEW WORLD

As people began to travel from continent to continent, Asians saw Europeans for the first time. Europeans saw Africans. After Columbus came to the New World, Native Americans saw all three.

Something very special happened in America. It was one of the first places where Native Americans, Africans, Asians, and Europeans *had* to learn to live side by side. America became the world's first truly diverse land. Yet at first everyone did not live "happily ever after." Many people were treated unfairly simply because of *what* they were, not *who* they were. To this day we keep trying to get things right.

A BROKEN PROMISE?

Our nation was born with the promise of liberty, justice, and freedom for all, but the people who wrote our nation's laws were worried. What if people coming from other lands did not understand "freedom"? What if they used our freedom to overthrow the government and take control? What if these newcomers did not fit in?

America made some mistakes as it grew. We may be the oldest working democracy in the world, but we are also one of the youngest countries, and our country is still learning—just like you!

STAY AWAY!

Laws were written to keep rights away from certain groups of people who wanted to move here. Some men and women who really wanted to live here were sent home. Others, who were allowed to stay, could not vote or share in the benefits of being American citizens.

This artist drew a picture of people from many lands sitting side by side, sharing in the riches of America. In truth it was hard to make that happen.

UNCLE SAM'S THANKSGIVING DINNER.

As more and more people began to arrive in the United States, it became important to figure out a way to keep track of the newcomers and to decide if their arrival would help our new country... or hurt it.

FROM THERE TO HERE

Moving to a new country is a hard choice to make. You can't just hop on a plane or climb aboard a ship and go. You need permission, and not everyone is welcome here. There are rules that you must follow and papers that you must have.

AMERICA, THE GROWING

In the years after the American Revolution, only a few people came to live in America. Crossing an ocean was dangerous! But beginning in 1814, as years of war ended, the trickle turned into a flood. By 1820, word in Europe was spreading: America was a land of opportunity! Soon ships crammed with newcomers began to dock daily. As the new arrivals walked down the gangplanks clutching every possession they owned, they wondered, "What will happen next?"

FIRST STEPS

Imagine coming to a strange place where you cannot understand what people are saying. You must quickly learn a new language. You will have to stay with family or friends until you can find a place to live. You need to find work or a school to attend. Over time you may have to learn to be **bilingual** (by-lin-gwill)—speaking English, even though you still speak your native tongue at home. And you will have to get used to a different way of life—an unfamiliar culture with new foods, holidays, and ways of doing things.

IN SEARCH OF A GREEN CARD

Today most newcomers arrive with a booklet called a **passport**. Many of them must also get a **visa** (VEE-za), which tells how long they can stay and what they can do—work, study, or just visit.

If you come from another country, you are called an **alien** (ALE-ee-in)—a fancy word for someone from far away. If you want to stay in America, you must get a resident alien card, nicknamed a "**green card**." These cards (which are beige, by the way) are very hard to get. People who cannot get a card may feel they have no choice but to stay here anyway. If they do that, they have broken the law. They are then here **illegally** (ill-EE-gul-ly), which means "against the law."

WELCOME (AND NOT WELCOME) IN AMERICA

THE "CHINESE WALL" AROUND THE UNITED STATES of AMERICA.

THROWING DOWN THE LADDER BY WHICH THEY ROSE.

This drawing from 1870 shows Americans pushing ladders down as Chinese people try to climb up a make-believe wall around America.

Sometimes things that are legal can be wrong. Slavery was once legal. Women voting was illegal. Laws change as life in America changes. One set of laws that have changed many times are laws about who should be allowed to live in the United States.

If everyone who wanted to come to America came, there might not be enough jobs to go around. There might not be enough housing or schools. And there *are* some people who may wish to harm us. How do we decide whom to allow in?

In America's early days, we needed people to come and work here, but in later years some people became afraid of folks who looked different. They did not understand that diversity was a good thing, and people from some countries were told they could not come here. Our government is *still* trying to make good rules about whom to let in. America still offers suffering people **asylum** (us-EYE-lum)—a safe haven in a stormy world. Yet many people who **immigrate**—move to a new country hoping to settle there—face problems. If they do not follow the rules, they can be **deported**—sent back to the country they tried to leave.

FIRST STEPS IN A NEW LAND

For many years two tiny islands—one in New York and one in California—were the first stop for millions of people moving to America by sea. Would they be welcome here? Would they find work? Were the streets really paved with gold?

FAR FROM HOME

A hundred years ago, newcomers to America spent weeks, and sometimes months, getting here. When they arrived, dirty, tired, and scared, the first thing they had to do was wait some more. People stood packed shoulder to shoulder in long lines as they waited to see an immigration officer. A babble of voices speaking dozens of different languages and dialects filled the air. Finally it was time to talk to an immigration officer.

AN EXAM TO PASS

"Do you have any money? Do you have a job? Where will you live? Do you have family here?" So many questions! To make sure they had the right answers, many families "practiced" their answers before they arrived, coached by friends or family who had come before. After the interview it was time for a medical exam. That scared most people more than the ocean crossing had! Eyes were examined. Lungs were listened to. One cough could mean "no entry."

One of America's most famous immigrants lives in New York harbor. She's a 450,000 pound lady with size 879 shoes! The Statue of Liberty came here from France in 1885—in 214 crates. After she was put together, she became a beautiful symbol of America's promise of welcome to the world.

FIRST STOP: AN ISLAND

Between 1880 and 1930, more than 27 million people moved to the United States. Twenty million came through Ellis Island, and one million more passed through Angel Island. Some people found out (the hard way) that America did not always welcome people from every land.

ELLIS ISLAND NEW YORK

Sailing past the Statue of Liberty must have been a wonderful, yet scary sight. America was so close!

One man wrote, *"The boat anchored at mid-bay and then they tendered us on the ship to Ellis Island…We got off the boat… you got your bag in your hand and went right into the building. Ah, that day there must have been about five to six thousand people. Jammed! I remember it was August. Hot as a pistol, and I'm wearing my long-johns, and my heavy Irish tweed suit."*

Finally the dreaded medical exam and the long wait were over. A few people were held and sent back to Europe, but most headed to New York City and then on to places where their families or friends had already settled.

The streets of America were *not* paved with gold, yet many had taken their first steps on free soil. Now the new arrivals had to learn to make a life in a new land.

ANGEL ISLAND CALIFORNIA

For many, Angel Island was a place of heartbreak—a place where some people from parts of Asia discovered that they were not welcomed in America.

The Chinese had first come in the 1850s, but during hard times in the 1870s, a lot of folks blamed the Chinese for taking too many jobs. Soon after, America wrote new immigration laws based on race and nationality. In 1882 the United States passed a law called the Chinese Exclusion Act. People from China could no longer move here! For some, Angel Island became a hated place where they were held for months, only to be sent home. A poem carved on one wall read, *"…I ate wind and tasted waves for more than twenty days. Fortunately, I arrived safely on the American continent. I thought I could land in a few days. How was I to know I would become a prisoner suffering in the wooden building?"*

From Angel Island you can see the city of San Francisco, but for some people of Asian birth, that view was as close as they ever came to America.

From the outside Ellis Island looked like a fun place, but on the inside a huge waiting room was packed with thousands of smelly, tired people!

WHO ARE WE?

Perhaps your ancestors sailed here 300 years ago. Maybe your parents just stepped off an airplane last year. These are the places from which we came.

PUSHED OR PULLED

By the mid 1800s, the American colonies had become states, and our nation was growing quickly. For the next century and a half, boatloads of people were drawn to our shores. Some were "pulled" here—drawn by the promises of religious freedom or plenty of jobs. Others were "pushed" from their homes by war, hunger, and poverty.

WHERE DID WE COME FROM: 1820 TO TODAY

1820 was a very important year. That was the first year the American government began to count the people coming here and record the places they were leaving. Since that year more than 65 million people have immigrated to America. Most came from Europe. That's because the original thirteen colonies of the United States had been settled by folks from that continent.

These days people from Asia, the Americas, and Africa are frequent arrivals.

All data is as of 2000

NUMBER OF PEOPLE (IN MILLIONS) WHO HAVE COME HERE FROM 1820-2000

- 40
- 35
- 30
- 25
- 20
- 15
- 10
- 5
- 0

Europe

North America

INCLUDES:
Mexico
Canada
Central America
The Caribbean

Asia

South America

Before 1820 about 500,000 Africans came directly to the U.S. as slaves, but about ten million were brought to the Caribbean, and Central and South America.

Africa

Oceania

| almost 39 million | almost 14 million | almost 9.5 million | almost 3.5 million | almost 1 million since slavery ended | almost 300,000 |

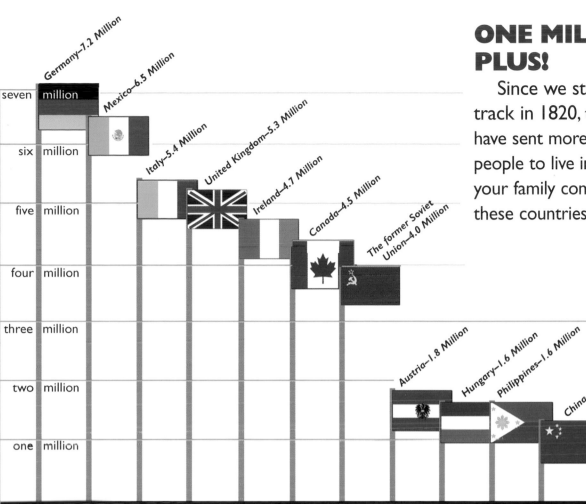

Germany—7.2 Million
Mexico—6.5 Million
Italy—5.4 Million
United Kingdom—5.3 Million
Ireland—4.7 Million
Canada—4.5 Million
The former Soviet Union—4.0 Million
Austria—1.8 Million
Hungary—1.6 Million
Philippines—1.6 Million
China—1.4 Million
Sweden—1.2 Million
India—1.0 Million

seven million
six million
five million
four million
three million
two million
one million

ONE MILLION PLUS!

Since we started keeping track in 1820, twelve countries have sent more than a million people to live in America. Did your family come from any of these countries?

All data is as of 2000

THE TOP TEN

Where did most immigrants settle in the early 21st century?*

1. **California**
2. **New York**
3. **Florida**
4. **Texas**
5. **New Jersey**
6. **Illinois**
7. **Massachusetts**
8. **Virginia**
9. **Washington, DC**
10. **Maryland**

*Between 2000 and 2005

HOW ARE WE CHANGING?

By the time you are a grown-up, America will have changed a lot. In the year 2000, about three-quarters of us had our family roots in Europe, but by the year 2030, almost half of all Americans will have ties to Latin America, Africa, or Asia.

Native American
Asian
African
Latino
European

2000

Native American
Asian
African
European
Latino

2030

By the time the first European explorer set foot on America's shores, millions of people already lived here—300 different proud, strong, diverse nations in North America alone. The first Americans built towns, roads, and complex governments. They left a lasting mark on the land.

AMERICA'S FIRST PEOPLE

A Navajo girl

An Inuit girl

A Sioux boy dressed for a festival

THE FIRST AMERICANS

For a long time historians believed that the first Americans walked here over a frozen chunk of land between Asia and what is now Alaska about 12,000 years ago during the last Ice Age—a time when it was very cold and the oceans began to freeze. New findings tell a different story. People may have first come to North and South Americas by boat about 20,000 years ago.

SACRED SOIL

Many Native Americans believe that their ancestors have always been here. Their sacred stories, much like the story of Adam and Eve, tell of them being created here. But no matter how they got here, the country we live in today was shaped by these first people. More than half of our states have Indian names, such as Illinois and Texas. Many of our big cities and highways are on native sites and paths. We use Indian words, like "skunk" and "chipmunk." Even the idea of "united states" was inspired in part by a united group of six nations—the Iroquois League.

A Powhatan village in Virginia

A Pueblo village in New Mexico

16

DIFFERENT WAYS, DIFFERENT LIVES

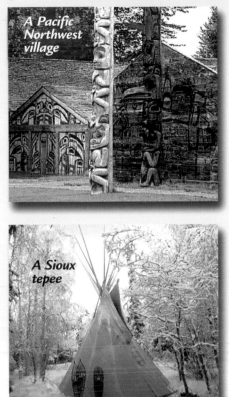

A Pacific Northwest village

A Sioux tepee

Many people think that all Indians lived in tepees, wore feathers in their hair, and hunted wild animals for their food. WRONG! Depending on where they lived, groups did things in their own special ways. Some lived in large towns. Some survived by farming or fishing.

More than 140 different languages were spoken in what is now the United States. People dressed differently and lived in different types of homes, depending on the region where they lived. They made beautiful weavings, jewelry, and pottery. They told great stories and made wonderful music. But their way of life would change forever after 1492, the year Christopher Columbus came to America.

A thousand years ago a city now called Cahokia Mounds (near what is modern-day St. Louis) was home to between 10,000 and 20,000 people—more than lived in London, England, at that time.

THE FIRST DARK DAYS

American Indians suffered terribly when Europeans first began to come to America. For one thing, the Europeans didn't know it, but they carried smallpox germs. Because the First Americans had never been exposed to this very deadly disease or other germs the Europeans carried, they had no immunity. That means their bodies could not fight off the germs. Entire villages were wiped out. Two out of every three American Indians on the continent died! In some places those who did not die became slaves. They were forced to clear fields for the colonists who had pushed them off their very own lands.

This painting shows a European who has accidentally spread smallpox germs by coughing on a First American.

17

WHEN AMERICA MET EUROPE

Major American Indian nations

This painting shows Squanto, a Pawtuxet Indian, teaching the Pilgrims a new way to plant crops in the rocky New England soil.

TRAILS OF TEARS

The new European settlers would not have survived without help from the Indians. The First Americans knew where to find safe, healthy places to live, understood the land, and knew the best crops to grow. Instead of thanking them, in 1830, the United States passed a law called the "Indian Removal Act." The European-Americans wanted more land. All the Indian nations east of the Mississippi River—even ones who lived peacefully—had to leave their homes and go west. In the winter of 1838-39, 14,000 men, women, and children walked 1,200 miles across five states where they were forced to live on **reservations** (rez-ur-VAY-shunz)—marked-off land in some of the worst parts of the country. Surviving was a struggle, and it was all too easy to lose hope.

Close to 4,000 people died on this long cold walk of sorrow. Is it any wonder American Indians called it the Trail of Tears?

THE CODE TALKERS

In spite of being mistreated, American Indians were still willing to help build and protect our nation by fighting bravely in America's wars. Their unique **heritage** even helped the United States win World War II, the worst war we have ever fought.

The United States needed a code—a way to send messages to our troops that the enemy could not break. The U.S. military turned to the Navajo because their language uses tones as well as words, and is impossible to write down. The "Code Talkers" went into enemy territory and relayed messages in their native language. The enemy could not break the code. Without the Code Talkers, the war would have lasted a lot longer, and many more people would have died.

Navajo Code Talkers were sworn to secrecy. Even their families did not know what they did in the war. Twenty years after World War II was over, the government finally told the world about their heroism.

THE SKYWALKERS

America is famous for its huge skyscrapers. When the first towering buildings started to go up in the 1920s, Mohawk iron workers became famous for "walking the high steel" on many of our most famous skyscrapers and bridges. Because they had no fear of heights, they could walk on the narrowest beams even on windy days, carrying heavy loads as they worked 100 floors up without safety belts!

A BRIGHT FUTURE

Today more than two million American Indians live in the United States. They have tried to hold on to their traditions while working to rebuild their ancestors' tribes. They still must fight against **prejudice** *(PREH-ju-dis)*—people not liking others simply because they are different. But slowly America's first nations are reclaiming a place for themselves.

One hundred stories up without a safety belt or a hard hat, this American Indian steelworker stood on a girder high atop New York's Empire State Building, built in 1930.

What do you think of when you hear the word *Africa*? Wild animals? Jungles? Africa has so much more! There are vast grasslands, huge deserts, and big cities. Today there are more than fifty different countries, each with its own special traditions.

COMING FROM AFRICA

A girl in Mali

A boy in Morocco

A girl in Kenya

OUT OF AFRICA

People have been living in Africa longer than any other place on Earth—some believe more than a million years! It is no wonder that Africa was home to some of the world's greatest **civilizations** (siv-uh-la-ZAY-shunz).

Egypt's amazing pyramids rose up in North Africa. Timbuktu, in the empire of Mali, was a great center of learning. Africa has gold, silver, and precious minerals. Caravans led by merchants and traders from faraway lands came to buy and sell things. The people of Africa—the Mende, Zulu, Yoruba, and Edo, to name just a few—were skilled farmers, fishermen, artists, and scholars.

THE EARLIEST EXPLORERS?

Some historians think that African boats may have visited the Americas long before Christopher Columbus ever set foot here! A natural current runs across the Atlantic Ocean from the middle of Africa almost directly to the place where Columbus landed in 1492. In the years after that famous trip, Africans came to the Americas with Spanish explorers, but their fate began to change in the early 1500s.

The Egyptians built some of the world's most amazing architecture, such as these 4,000 year-old pyramids.

Timbuktu's great mosque was built in Mali more than 500 years ago.

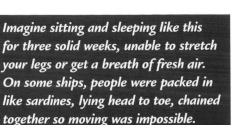

CHAINS OF SADNESS

Sadly, slavery has been around for centuries. All over the world, prisoners of war often became slaves. Slaves are bought and sold and often treated badly—forced to work for others against their will. The European colonists in America needed strong people to work on their new plantations and farms, but the Native Americans were dying from smallpox and measles. European and American merchants looked to Africa for workers and quickly built a vast business trading in human beings. In the 1500s the first enslaved Africans were brought to the Americas to work on sugar plantations in South America and the Caribbean, and later were taken to what is now the U.S.A.

THE MIDDLE PASSAGE

How did the slave trade happen? The Europeans hired raiders to capture African men and women and built forts to hold them captive. They sent ships to bring their prisoners to the Americas. Some African traders and kingdoms took part in the slave trade but most Africans tried to protect themselves. Many fought back. Meanwhile, the demand for unpaid workers in the Americas grew, and wars broke out in parts of Africa. More Africans got drawn into the slave trade and it became harder and harder for African communities to protect themselves. Millions of Africans were enslaved and millions more died.

The trip from Africa to America—the middle part of a triangular route connecting three continents—became known as the Middle Passage. It was a nightmare! People were packed so tightly that they could not lie down to sleep. Awful diseases killed millions along the way. Others jumped overboard, choosing drowning instead of living as slaves!

The almost ten million Africans who were forced into slavery could not bring their possessions with them, but they always carried their traditions, their music, and customs in their hearts. They never, ever forgot their roots.

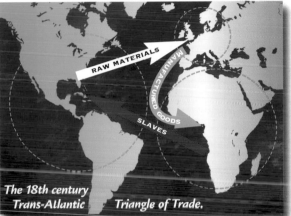

The 18th century Trans-Atlantic Triangle of Trade.

RAW MATERIALS
MANUFACTURED GOODS
SLAVES

Ships sailed from Europe to Africa with manufactured goods such as textiles and guns. In Africa these were traded for human cargo. The ships then sailed to the Americas, where the enslaved Africans were traded for sugar, cotton, tobacco, molasses, and rum, which the ships took back to Europe.

WHEN AFRICA MET AMERICA

FROM DAWN 'TIL DARK

In 1619 a boat carrying about 20 Africans docked in Jamestown, Virginia. They came as **indentured** (in-DEN-shurd) **servants**, people who would work for five to seven years, often in exchange for a small piece of land. More Africans followed. After a few years their European bosses began to think, "Why bother giving these people freedom? Why not just make them slaves forever?" A slave had to work long hours for no pay and could be bought and sold. In time the bosses decided that the workers' children would become slaves too, so there was always a fresh supply of workers. A terrible cycle of evil—people owning other people—soon fell into place.

Slaves rose before dawn and worked rain or shine until darkness fell. They had no hope for a better future. In a country based on freedom, it was a horrible way to live. What would America have been like without the Africans? Our country grew rich because of all the their hard work! They had been skilled farmers in Africa and knew how to grow crops such as rice. They were expert weavers and craftspeople. People from coastal Africa were great boatbuilders and sailors. They helped to clothe, feed, and earn money for our struggling new nation.

Not every African in America was a slave. There were free people of color in some areas, especially in the North where the economy did not depend as much on slave labor. There were even a few African Americans who became slave-owners themselves. Still, by the 1800s, the color of a person's skin began to be seen as proof that he or she was probably a slave. In spite of that, Africans in America clung tightly to the hope that somehow, one day, they and their children would be free.

A cotton plantation was a busy place. It took many hands to pick, clean, and get the cotton ready to be sold.

LET MY PEOPLE GO

Sadly, America became the place where a new chapter in the story of slavery was written. It was the first place on Earth where the law said that if your mother was a slave, then so were you. It took real courage to speak out against slavery. A person could be beaten or killed for escaping or for trying to help someone who had, yet many were willing to die trying.

PORTRAITS IN DIGNITY

Harriet Tubman, **Frederick Douglass**, and **Sojourner Truth** risked death to end slavery. As they spoke out about the horrors of slave life, people began to listen. By the 1860s the time was at hand for people of color finally to be set free—to at last have a chance for life, liberty, and the pursuit of happiness.

BROKEN CHAINS

In 1865 the Civil War finally ended slavery in America, but African Americans still faced a bitter struggle. They longed to be treated with dignity. Instead they faced decades of **discrimination** *(dis-crim-in-A-shun)*—being turned down for jobs, houses, a chance to vote, and even seats on the bus. The ugliness of slavery left a painful scar that we are still trying to heal.

A hundred years after the Civil War ended, a new generation of leaders, such as **Martin Luther King, Jr.**, **Rosa Parks**, and **Malcolm X,** went to work to help people of color gain the rights they deserved.

HEADS HELD HIGH

In spite of hundreds of years of being treated badly, African Americans have made huge contributions to life in America, from the foods we eat to the music we dance to. These days people from Africa are coming to America willingly—eager to find good jobs and a safe place to raise their families.

Memories of the terrible years of slavery are starting to fade, but we must never forget the brave men and women who made sure that no person would ever own another.

Harriet Tubman (1820-1913) was a wisp of a woman, but that didn't stop her from building the "Underground Railroad." It wasn't a train or a tunnel. Instead, Tubman found safe houses and hiding places for runaway slaves that brought them from the South as far north as Canada.

Frederick Douglass (1817-1895) escaped from a cruel slavemaster and fled north, where he changed his name and began speaking about the horrors of slavery. In time he started a newspaper, The North Star, devoted to ending slavery.

Sojourner Truth (1797-1883) was a freed slave from New York, who claimed she heard heavenly voices urging her to speak out against slavery. She too was a wonderful speaker who opened people's eyes to slavery's horrors.

Martin Luther King, Jr. (1929-1968) gave his life to earn equal rights for African Americans. He believed that non-violence was the only way to achieve equality. He led boycotts, sit-ins, and marches, and his "I Have a Dream" speech touched millions.

COMING FROM ASIA

A girl from India

A boy from China

A girl from Jordan

LAND OF CONTRASTS

Take a close look at these children. They are all from Asia, but they do not look alike or dress alike. They do not speak the same languages, eat the same foods, or pray the same ways. Naturally, when people from their countries began to move to America, they brought all sorts of different ways of doing things.

BIG AND SMALL

If you look at a list of the ten countries with the most people, seven of them are in Asia. China and India top the list. Asia has island nations like Japan and the Philippines.

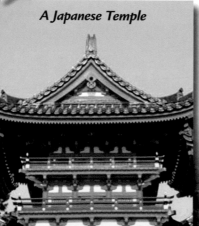

A Japanese Temple

Asia has the world's tallest, snowiest mountains. There are also the hot, dry nations of the Middle East, such as Iran, Jordan, Israel, and Iraq. The Asian continent is truly a land of diversity.

Asia is the biggest continent and home to almost fifty countries. Two out of every three people on Earth live in Asia.

Sadly, there have been many wars there and too many times when there was not enough to eat. People had to leave their homes to find work, food, and most of all, peace.

The Great Wall of China stretches for 2,150 miles. That is the distance from Washington D.C. to the California border.

India's Taj Mahal is one of the most famous buildings in the world.

Southeast Asia is a tropical wonderland.

Five-mile-high Mount Everest in Nepal is the tallest peak on Earth.

ACROSS THE PACIFIC

People from Asia have made great scientific discoveries, created beautiful artworks, and invented wonderful things such as ice cream and paper. Why leave such a place? In spite of Asia's riches, its people have faced great sadness such as wars, earthquakes, and floods that have forced them from their homes.

GOLD MOUNTAIN

In the middle of the 1800s, two things happened in two far-apart places. In 1848 gold was found in California. At about the same time China was hit by floods and famine, and people were starving to death! Soon stories began to swirl through Chinese villages—tales about mountains of gold in America. Many people, especially young men, sailed off to California, promising their families they would return home as rich men.

Other Asian people—the Japanese, Koreans, and people from the Philippines—would follow in the years to come, drawn by the promise of a chance to work hard and prosper in return.

Many of the world's religions started in Asia. The Holy Land, an area in the Middle East, was the birthplace of Judaism, Christianity, and Islam. Asia is also the home of the Buddhist, Hindu, Shinto, and Sikh faiths. Almost five billion people all over the world now belong to one of these seven religions.

Surprisingly, these religions have a lot in common. They all preach lessons of respect and honor, but all too often people have used religion as a reason to hurt others. The fact is, the world's faiths share many of the same basic values, such as charity and kindness toward all beings, both great and small.

THE BIRTHPLACE OF FAITH

WHEN ASIA MET AMERICA

GOLD MOUNTAIN

The Chinese called America *Gam Saan*—"Gold Mountain," but when they got here, they did not find much gold. Instead, like most people "pushed" to America, they found a strange and difficult life. Many tried working as miners for a few years, but hardly anyone grew rich. Soon they were forced to find other work as farmers, fishermen, laundrymen, and especially construction workers.

WORKING ON THE RAILROAD

In 1863 work began on an almost-impossible task. A railroad was being planned to link the east and west coasts of America, but there was a big problem. A mountain range blocked the way. The newly arrived Chinese were desperate for jobs, so thousands of men began the harsh work of blasting through rock to lay the tracks for a transcontinental railroad.

It was hard and dangerous work. The men dug and blasted in summer's heat and winter's blizzards, all for less than one dollar a day. That was much less than Irish workers were paid to do the same exact job. At first the work-bosses disliked the Chinese workers, but when they saw how hard they labored under terrible conditions, their attitudes changed and they grew to respect them.

This great railroad was built by one of the first diverse workforces in American history—mostly Chinese and Irish, with help from Native Americans and African Americans along the way. Thanks to them all, as one final spike was hammered in on May 10, 1869, America was finally linked from sea to sea.

Blasting tunnels through the mountains was very dangerous. Men were lowered over the sides in baskets where they chipped at the rock, planted dynamite, lit fuses, and hoped to be pulled to safety before the explosions!

At first only men came to America, but in time families joined their dads, like this mom and child in 1900.

It snowed so much in the mountains, the workers had to build long snow tunnels so the trains could move through the snowiest areas.

LEAVING JAPAN

People from Japan began arriving in America around 1885, "pushed" out by huge taxes and not enough farmlands at home, and "pulled" by the promise of wages six times higher in the U.S.A. Many came to Hawaii to work on sugar plantations or to California as farmhands, but they faced terrible discrimination. Still they worked hard and made sure that their children got good educations. Like the Chinese Americans, they too believed that doing well in school was their kids' ticket out of a life of hard labor.

WAR NO MORE

People came from other lands in Asia. In 1950 war broke out in Korea and split the country in two. America became involved, and many Koreans fled to the United States. In the 1970s an awful war ripped apart Vietnam and Laos. In Cambodia a cruel leader began killing anyone who didn't agree with him. More than two million people fled from Southeast Asia. Thousands also arrived from countries in the Middle East, such as Syria and Lebanon, fleeing civil war and religious unrest. Leaving home meant life!

Some Asian refugees had no money to buy a boat or plane ticket, so they pulled their houses apart and built boats from their walls and roofs! Many of these home-made boats broke apart at sea, and thousands drowned trying to escape to a safe place.

FRIEND OR FOE?

How would you feel if you were told you had to leave your home *this instant* and live behind barbed wire simply because of where your grandparents were born? By the 1940s Japanese Americans had become U.S. citizens and built homes and businesses. All that changed when Japan bombed our naval base at Pearl Harbor in Hawaii in 1941.

America went to war against Japan (and Germany). Our government ordered 120,000 Japanese Americans—half of them kids—to **internment** (*in-TURN-mint*) **camps**. Families lost their homes and jobs. For the next four years they lived in shacks in the middle of nowhere, even though they had nothing to do with the war. It was so unfair! We were at war with Germany too, but we did not round up people of German descent and send *them* to special camps. Almost fifty years later our government finally apologized to the Japanese Americans, who lost so much.

Manzanar was the biggest internment camp. It had rows and rows of prison barracks, which became "home" for four long years.

PROSPERITY CALLS

One of the largest groups to come from Asia are people from the Philippines, which was once controlled by America. They left hoping to get better jobs. People from India and Pakistan have also flocked here. Many were gifted scientists, engineers, doctors, and nurses. Moving to a new country is always tough, but these people brought much-needed skills. They have worked hard, and most have done well in America.

COMING FROM EUROPE

Europe is one of the smallest continents, yet it is packed with more than forty countries. It was here that empires grew and kings and queens fought on battlegrounds that soon stretched across the sea.

A girl from Ireland

A boy from Spain

A boy from Russia

NEW WORLD, NEW DREAMS

More people in the United States today trace their roots back to Europe than to any other continent. Why did so many leave their homes for an unknown future in America? For many years the "Old World" was a world of overcrowded cities, crop failures, political unrest, poverty, and religious discrimination.

A Cathedral in France

Today Europe has many beautiful cities such as London, Paris, and Rome, but for hundreds of years, kings and queens got rich at the expense of their people. Europe's rulers were often at war and always needed *more* money, *more* land, and *more* gold to build bigger castles and grander churches. That was why they wanted to set up **colonies**— groups of people living far from home, yet still ruled by their mother country. In America's early years the "New World" was all about money and power!

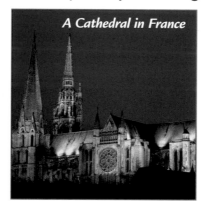

A crowded town in Spain

17th century Dutch colonists grew wealthy trading with American Indians.

LET'S SWAP

When people from different continents met, the world changed. New plants grew, and strange animals grazed where they had never been seen before.

FROM EUROPE, AFRICA, AND ASIA

horses
cattle
pigs
sheep
goats
chickens

oats
melon
rice
coffee
bananas
sugarcane
barley
olives

wheat
clover
dandelions
daisies

FROM THE AMERICAS

turkeys
llamas
alpacas
guinea Pigs

corn
potatoes
beans

tobacco
peanuts
squash
peppers
pomatoes
pumpkins
pineapples
vanilla
cacao (chocolate)
chicle (chewing gum)
manioc (tapioca)
avocados
guavas
papayas

LEAVING HOME

Within a few years of Columbus' trip, the kings and queens of Europe were carving America up like a Thanksgiving turkey! But each nation had a different idea about how to proceed. **Spain** sent soldiers to search for gold. **France** sent trappers to gather valuable animal skins. **The Netherlands** saw America as a huge business and formed trading companies. **England** sent families—fathers, mothers, and children—to start farms. That was smart. People *wanted* to be with their families. England soon had lots of "roots" put down in America. That is one reason America ended up as an English-speaking nation, not Spanish or Dutch.

MANY MILLIONS

Life was rough at first. There wasn't enough to eat. The weather was often brutal and the work hard, but more and more people came. Soon there were enough Europeans living here to encourage craftspeople and small shop owners to come also. Newcomers wrote to their families, "In America, everyone is free. Everyone has food." Of course, that wasn't exactly true, but over the next 300 years, more than 35 million people left Europe, crossed the Atlantic, and settled in America.

WHEN EUROPE MET AMERICA

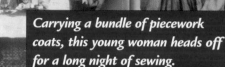

WHY NOT LICENSE HOME WORK

Carrying a bundle of piecework coats, this young woman heads off for a long night of sewing.

THERE ARE NEVER ENOUGH INSPECTORS TO PREVENT DIRT FILTH AND DISEASE

HOME WORK MEANS LONG HOURS LOW WAGES LITTLE PROTECTION FOR THE WORKERS IT ALSO DRAGS DOWN SHOP WAGES

WORK DONE IN THESE TENEMENTS GOES TO EVERY STATE IN THE UNION

A NATIONAL MENACE NEEDS A NATIONAL CURE

LEAVING HARD TIMES...

No food. No work. No freedom. These are all very bad things. In the 1800s, people kept flocking to America in bad times, and good times as well. In the 1900s two terrible world wars began in Europe. Millions more fled from Germany, Austria-Hungary, Russia, and the countries of Central Europe. The United States opened its arms to help these **refugees** *(ref-you-GEES)*—people seeking shelter from the horror of war.

FINDING HARD TIMES

After the first joyous hours in America, reality set in for the newcomers. Where would they live? How could they earn enough money to feed their families? New arrivals often ended up living in crowded **tenements** *(TEN-uh-mintz)*—awful apartments that often had rats, no fresh air or sunlight, and bad plumbing. They found whatever work they could. Many scrimped by doing piecework at home. Everyone, even five-year olds, sewed or tied strings to tags, for pennies a day! Little boys sold newspapers on street corners, and little girls worked in factories until laws were finally passed to end child labor, making it easier for kids to get decent educations.

SETTLING IN

Kids quickly got used to life in their new country. Most went to school, learned English, and became "Americanized." It was not so easy for their parents, who clung to their old customs. They read newspapers printed in their native tongues and sought the company of people from their homelands. But one thing most immigrant moms and dads had in common, no matter where they came from, was the hope their kids would learn to read and write. Still when money was tight, boys and girls often got pulled from school and sent to work.

Not every immigrant was poor or uneducated. When wars tore Europe apart in the 1900s, great people like Albert Einstein fled. Doctors, musicians, scientists, and artists flocked to America.

STREETS PAVED WITH GOLD?

Two countries saw more than ten million of their people leave for America over a very short period of time. Immigrants from other countries such as Germany, Russia, and Sweden shared their experiences.

IRELAND'S BAD POTATOES

In Ireland in the fall of 1845, farmers began to harvest their potato crops and found they had turned black and slimy. The Irish depended on potatoes for food, but their plants were all dying. Over the next few years more than a million people starved to death because there wasn't enough to eat.

For many Irish families, America was their last hope. They arrived on boats where so many died they were called "coffin ships." If they survived the trip, they took any jobs they could find, but the signs on some businesses read, "No Irish Need Apply." Still America was growing. It needed railroads and bridges. Cities were growing, too, and needed police and firefighters. Irish workers began to fill those jobs.

In time Irish Americans became very involved in politics and ran for public office. A hundred years after the potatoes first rotted, Irish Americans were governing the very towns and cities they had moved to when they first fled from famine.

ITALY'S LITTLEST WORKERS

Between 1876 and 1924, more than six million Italians headed to America in search of jobs. Most came from southern Italy, where they worked as peasants or share-croppers—farmers who pay for renting small bits of land with a portion of the crops grown on that land. There were hardly any schools to attend, and by the age of nine, most kids worked full-time in the fields. Parents dreamed of a better life for their kids.

In America the new arrivals settled with other Italians in neighborhoods called "Little Italies." Because they had little schooling, many ended up as laborers, but they had a tradition of working hard and took great pride in caring for one another. They formed clubs that lent money and helped people find jobs. They stuck together, and as their kids went to school and got good educations, the Italians began to settle in and prosper.

The Homestead Act of 1862 promised free land to people willing to move west. Over two million European immigrants boarded trains and settled on the Great Plains, bringing Old World farming styles to that part of the country.

NEIGHBORS WHO CAME TO STAY

NORTH AND SOUTH

As people from Canada, Mexico, and Cuba crossed America's borders the states near those borders changed. Canadian workers filled mill towns in Maine. "Little Havana" sprang up in the middle of Miami as Cubans flocked there, and today more than half the people in Miami speak Spanish. Tex-Mex cuisine and Caribbean music soon became American favorites.

Mexican cowboys were some of the very first cowboys. After the Civil War, they were joined by freed African Americans.

After the Mexican-American War ended in 1848, Mexico was forced to give up the land in the light area. The yellow area is the Gasdon Purchase of 1853—land bought from Mexico because a railroad was planned for the area.

HOME ON THE RANGE

Today Mexican Americans are one of the biggest ethnic groups in the United States. Many of them ended up living in America after war with Mexico changed our borders in the mid-1800s. As Texans of Mexican descent like to say, "We never crossed the border. The border crossed us."

Mexicans played a big part in developing the West. There were wealthy ranchers in the Rio Grande area, and farmers growing all sorts of crops. Mexicans were also some of the first cowboys. The word "cowboy" comes from the Mexican *vaquero* (vah-KEH-row). In Spanish, a *vaca* is a cow. The vaqueros herded cattle on large ranches. After the Civil War, as the demand for beef grew, the legend of the cowboy grew along with it.

The Mexican cowboys brought their special styles of saddle, leather chaps, and wide-brimmed hats, along with their riding, roping, and ranching skills. Today's rodeos, with fancy rope tricks and bucking-bronco riding, were all inspired by the skills of the Mexican cowboys.

Mexican cowboys sometimes call themselves charros. This family is dressed for a festival.

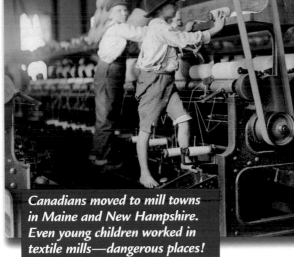

Canadians moved to mill towns in Maine and New Hampshire. Even young children worked in textile mills—dangerous places!

MAKING ENDS MEET

What happens when people come to America without a good education? They have to take jobs that pay very little. In the early 1900s French-Canadians in America found jobs in textile and paper mills. New arrivals from Mexico and Central America became **migrant** *(MY-grant)* farm workers. Migrants move a lot, picking fruit and vegetables.

The Bracero Program (1942-1964) let Mexicans work on farms in the U.S because there were not enough workers after World War II. More than four million people legally came here, for wages scorned by most Americans. For 20 years Mexican workers came and went legally until the laws changed, simply because the workers were no longer needed.

RIPE AND READY

These days most of the fruit and vegetable crops in the United States are picked by migrants, many of whom have come to America illegally. They travel from town to town, living in makeshift camps, working long hours for low pay. But not everyone struggles when he or she gets here. Some find fame and fortune!

Cesar Chavez, a Mexican American, spoke out against the bad treatment of migrant workers.

USA
37

CESAR E. CHAVEZ
2003

PLAY BALL

These days sports are one way talented folks from neighboring lands have grown rich in America. Canadians invented the sport of ice hockey, and Canadian players are some of the best around. Baseball attracts the talents of many athletes from the Caribbean. In Cuba and the Dominican Republic, baseball is a huge favorite. Today there are more Dominicans on America's major league baseball teams than any other ethnic group.

MARIANO
RIVERA 42

Mariano Rivera is just one of many ball players from the Dominican Republic.

COMING FROM SOUTH AMERICA

Cousins from Argentina

A boy from Brazil

A girl from Colombia

There is another America—South America. Twelve countries share this continent with the world's longest mountain chain, biggest rainforest, and driest desert. From the tropical north to the freezing cold south, *this* America is a place of amazing beauty.

GOLD AND GREED

Eight hundred years ago the Inca of Peru ruled over a vast empire in South America. They built amazing cities whose ruins still dazzle us to this day. But in the early 1500s the same sad fate that hit North America swept across South America too. Explorers from Spain and Portugal spread diseases that killed many of the native peoples, making it easy to take control.

South America had everything—fertile soil, a fine climate, and natural resources such as rubber, coffee, and of course silver and gold, so Spain and Portugal worked out a plan to divide up most of the continent. The Portuguese enslaved millions of Africans and put them to work on vast plantations in Brazil and for the next 350 years Spain and Portugal controlled the continent.

The Amazon River snakes across South America for more than 4,000 miles.

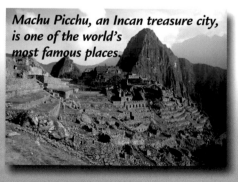
Machu Picchu, an Incan treasure city, is one of the world's most famous places.

Beautiful Rio de Janiero

FLYING TOWARDS PEACE

In the early 1800s, revolution came to South America. Inspired by the American and French revolutions, the people of South America pushed Spain and Portugal out. Some of the brand-new countries did well. Others struggled. Some countries, such as Argentina, were settled by millions of immigrants from Europe, much like the United States.

People from South America began moving to the U.S.A in large numbers about fifty years ago when the immigration rules changed and airplanes made getting here easier. By then people *wanted* to come because life had grown unstable in parts of South America. Presidents were elected, only to get pushed out by Army generals with guns and tanks.

In Argentina almost 10,000 people "disappeared" forever because they didn't agree with the generals. In some places money became worthless overnight. These days, Colombia, Ecuador, and Peru see the largest number of their people moving to the United States—all looking for peace, security, jobs, and a chance for a better life.

Guinea pigs are the cuddliest immigrants from South America!

The tango is one of the most famous dances in the world. It was first danced in Argentina.

HISPANIC OR LATINO: WHAT'S THE DIFFERENCE?

Hispania is the Latin word for Spain. If your ancestors came from Spain or a country that was settled by the Spanish, you might call yourself Hispanic.

What is a Latino or Latina? It's a way to describe Central and South American people from places where the languages are based on Latin. Latin is the "mother" language of Spanish, Portuguese (POR-chew-geez), French and Italian. A Latino doesn't have to be Spanish-speaking. Someone from Brazil, where they speak Portuguese, is a Latino, but not Hispanic. A person from Jamaica is not a Hispanic or a Latino since Jamaicans speak English.

What is a Chicano or Chicana? That name is sometimes used for a person of Mexican heritage who was born in the United States. Latinos are the largest and fastest growing group in the United States, and they are going to have a big impact on America's culture in the years to come.

Brazilian soccer star Pele is one of the biggest reasons the sport of soccer became so popular in the United States.

COMING FROM OCEANIA

A girl from Australia | A child from Fiji | A Samoan boy

A continent is a very large land mass. Australia is a continent, but it is also part of Oceania—the more than 20,000 beautiful islands that form a watery wonderland in the Pacific Ocean. Oceania spreads across an area larger than North and South America.

A kangaroo in Australia

THE LAND "DOWN UNDER"

That's what people often call Australia because it is entirely "down under" the **equator** *(ee-KWAY-tur)*—an imaginary line that circles the middle of the Earth. But there are also fourteen other countries in Oceania that spread across thousands of islands in the Pacific Ocean, some big and some tiny. These islands have been divided into three main groups—Polynesia, Melanesia, and Micronesia.

The people who live on the smaller islands are surrounded by water and live off the bounty of the sea. Naturally, they are great sailors. Some historians even believe that people from these islands came to the Americas long before Columbus. Could they have been some of the world's first explorers?

Two fishermen from Tahiti set off in an outrigger canoe— sturdy and stable in rough seas.

This modern-day Maori from New Zealand still holds true to the ways of his ancestors.

ALOHA

Hawaii, our fiftieth state, is 2,500 miles away from the United States mainland. It was first settled by people from Polynesia a thousand years ago. Hawaiians lived peacefully for hundreds of years until the 1800s when the first Americans of European ancestry arrived, determined to change the way the Hawaiians lived.

DO IT MY WAY

Missionaries (*MISH-un-air-eez*) are people who go to other lands to convince people to worship in *their* way. By now you know about the diseases that killed so many native peoples on the mainland of America. The same thing happened in Hawaii when the missionaries arrived in 1800. The missionaries did not know they brought diseases, but within a few short years more than 350,000 Hawaiians had died of illnessess to which they had no immunity.

Hula is a form of storytelling mixed with dance. It first came to the Hawaiian Islands with the Polynesians, who were the first to settle there.

ISLES OF DIVERSITY

With so many natives dead, the missionaries ended up owning many large plantations. They needed workers, so by 1900 more than forty percent of Hawaii's population came from Japan. People from three continents had met in Hawaii and that meeting led to the building of another land of diversity!

SURF'S UP

Surfing came to Hawaii with the arrival of settlers from Polynesia. It soon became an important part of the culture. Hawaiian royalty used surfing as a way to display their power. Kings rode waves on boards that were twice the size of boards owned by commoners, proving their strength by riding the biggest, scariest waves they could "catch."

Missionaries frowned on surfing. It took too much time away from praying! But somehow the sport survived, and in the early 1900s it made a come-back. In the 1920s, surfing demonstrations by Hawaiians in California started a new craze—*Surfing U.S.A.* What was once the sport of kings was now a part of American culture, touching everything from clothes to music.

Gidget

THE LITTLE GIRL WITH BIG IDEAS

a novel by

FREDERICK KOHNER

WHEN WAR CAME

America's fate became more closely wrapped up with Oceania's during World War II. Fierce fighting took place on many of the islands since they lay halfway between America and the Japanese enemy. After the war we kept military bases on some of the islands, such as Guam, which soon became United States **protectorates** (*pro-TEK-tuh-ritz*). These are weaker nations under the protection and partial control of a stronger nation. Because of this special status, it is sometimes easier for people from these places to come to America.

YUMMY FOODS FROM FAR AWAY

If you could never eat your favorite food again, you might be sad. So when people moved to America, they always tried to bring the plants or foods they loved with them. Once they were here, other folks tasted these new foods and loved them too!

Can you imagine life without these? These foods from faraway are all examples of diversity at work!

PEANUTS

Ground peanuts were a favorite of enslaved **Africans** who came to America. After George Washington Carver published his list of 360 things to do with peanuts, a dentist in St. Louis added oil to crushed peanuts to make peanut butter—a nourishing food for patients whose bad teeth made chewing hard.

CHOCOLATE & VANILLA

The **Mayans** and **Aztecs** in Mexico and Central America adored the beans of the cacao (ka-COW) trees. They also loved vanilla beans, which come from orchid plants that grow in rainforests. They used cacao beans for money as well as making a frothy, bitter drink. Spanish traders brought vanilla and cacoa beans to Europe, where they became a hit. In the early 1800s a **Dutch** chemist made chocolate into candy. Yum!

FRANKS & BURGERS

What's more all-American than a picnic with these two foods? Well, for starters, both dishes were named after two towns in **Germany**—Hamburg and Frankfurt. But it was in **England** in the late 1700s that the first recipe for "hamburgh sausage" first appeared in a cookbook.

DONUTS & COOKIES

Dutch immigrants used to fry pieces of bread dough in hot oil. Some say they twisted the bread into a knot—a dough-knot. Cookies are another Dutch treat, called *koekjes (cook-yes)* in Holland.

TACOS & TORTILLAS

Corn was a holy food to many American Indians. In **Mexico** in ancient times, corn, not bread or rice, was served at every meal. Tortillas, which are made from ground corn, make a perfect food holder.

ICE CREAM CONES

Many people think the **Chinese** invented ice cream about 1,000 years ago. Italian silk traders tasted the frosty treat and brought the recipe to Europe. Cones were "invented" by an **Italian-American** in the late 1800s, but they didn't catch on until 1904. That year a **Syrian-American** selling wafer cookies at a big fair rolled his wafers into cones to help the ice-cream vendor next door, who'd run out of dishes.

COFFEE

Many grownups like to start their mornings with a hot cup of this bitter drink. They have the farmers of **Ethiopia** (Ee-thee-OH-pee-uh) in Africa to thank. They were the ones who found that coffee keeps folks awake.

BAGELS

That crusty roll with a hole probably came to America from **Poland**, where Jewish bakers made big pretzels that were round instead of knotted. Americans added their own special touch by smearing cream cheese on top.

PIZZA

Pizza is the Italian word for "pie." Flat-breads with toppings such as cheese and onions were very popular in the southern parts of **Italy**. But before the Italians could make tomato sauce, tomato plants had to get *to* Italy *from* America.

ALL-AMERICAN FOOD

Not every good food comes from far away. American Indians have been eating tasty treats for thousands of years.

GOT GRITS?

In the 1500s, when the early explorers came ashore, the natives fed them hot bowls of *rockahominie (rock-a-HOM-a-nee)*, soft corn topped with salt and melted animal fat. We know them better as scrumptious grits.

MAPLE SYRUP & MORE

What would you pour on your pancakes if you didn't have syrup? The first Americans learned how to boil down maple tree sap to make this sweet treat. They also shared these treats with the Europeans: baked beans, cornbread, popcorn, squash, pecans, chile peppers, beef jerky, and sunflower seeds.

43

THE WIDE WORLD OF SPORTS

Baseball? It got its start in England. Football? Its roots go back to Italy. Soccer? It may have come from China. Even basketball was invented by a man who came from Canada.

Without diversity, recess would be very dull. Our favorite sports are based on games from far away.

BASEBALL

In **England**, school kids still play a 500-year-old game called *Rounders*. Our game of baseball grew from it. *Cricket* is another cool bat and ball game from England, which also has a lot in common with baseball. Folks from the Carribean love cricket and have brought it to America.

FOOTBALL

In **ancient Rome**, gladiators (*GLAD-ee-a-torz*) fought to the death over a small ball. That event grew into the sport of *rugby*—football without pads or helmets. American college kids loved the game but played too rough. In 1905 after bad head injuries and several deaths, the President of the United States asked the schools to make football safer, so helmets were added.

BASKETBALL

Basketball *was* first played in the U.S.A., but the man who invented it, Lawrence Naismith, was born in **Canada**. And in South America thousands of years ago, the ancient **Mayans** tossed small balls into *very* high hoops.

Yao (from China) takes on Shaquille O' Neal.

TENNIS

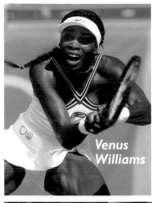
Venus Williams

In **France** about 800 years ago, folks started hitting a ball over a string with their hands, but the hard leather balls hurt, so wooden racquets were invented. They were too heavy, so a wood frame with strings came into play. The game quickly became a favorite of royal folks.

GOLF

Tiger Woods

Scotland, the land of bagpipes and kilts, brought us this very hard-to-play sport. The Scots have been playing golf since the 1400s. It is one of the few sports where the *lowest* score wins.

LACROSSE

College Lacrosse

Up in **Canada**, Native Americans have been playing *Baggataway* (Bag-uh-TA-wee) for centuries. Whole villages played at a time, and games could last for days. A **French** priest named it *lacrosse* because the stick looked like a bishop's staff.

SOCCER

Mia Hamm

Many places claim to have invented soccer. It was played in **ancient China** and during the Mayan period in **Peru**. The **English** formed football **associations** (*uh-so-see-A-shunz*). "Soccer" comes from a short part of that word—*soc.*

ICE HOCKEY

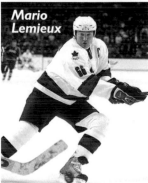
Mario Lemieux

As folks from **Ireland**, **England**, and **Scotland** came to **Canada** in the 1800s, they brought three games: *hurling, curling,* and *field hockey.* Canada is very cold in the winter, so a combination of all three games ended up as ice hockey.

THE OLYMPICS

Are you an athlete? That word comes from the Greek word *athlos*, which means "contest." The **ancient Greeks** gave us one of the best contests in the world—the Olympics. It all began in 776 B.C.E., when a group of swift runners came to a place called Olympia as part of a religious celebration.

FASTER! HIGHER! STRONGER!

Over time the number of events grew from a single foot race to include all sorts of sports. Today's winners get medals, but back then the winners got olive tree branches. There were no silver or bronze medals either, and losers were sometimes beaten with sticks!

For hundreds of years, sports fans came to Olympia to cheer for their favorite athletes until the games were banned after the Greek empire crumbled about two thousand years ago. In 1896 the first modern Olympics was held, and a great sports event was reborn.

FUN AND GAMES

Roll the dice. Make your move. Many of our favorite ways to play came from far away!

Today we play for fun, but in times past, great treasures and even kingdoms were sometimes won and lost on a roll of the dice or the shuffle of a deck.

Rainy days and long car rides would be really boring without these pastimes, which all came to America from other lands. Diversity equals fun!

PLAYING CARDS

The **Chinese** invented paper, and once they did that, playing cards followed. Their cards were carried to Spain by way of Arab traders from the **Islamic Empire**—a wealthy civilization that reached from Spain and Northern Africa to the Middle East. In the 1500s Gypsies may have spread them across Europe, but it was in England that our modern decks took shape. After all, who better to give us kings and queens?

CHESS

India gets the credit for this game, invented in the 6th century. They called it *Shatranj (sha-trandge)*. Their game had four sets of pawns, ships, horses, elephants, and kings. Arab traders brought the game to Spain and then to France, where four sets of playing pieces became two.

CHECKERS

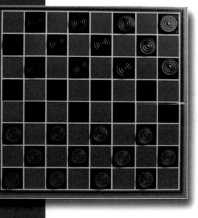

Two thousand years ago **Egyptians** played a game that is the grandpa of checkers. In many Arab countries a game called *El-Quirkat* grew from that Egyptian game. When the **Moors** (the peoples of **North Africa**) invaded Spain, they brought their game with them. Spain is close to France, which named the game *Alquerque (Al-kirk)*. They began playing it on a chess board. The French invented "kinging" and passed the game on to the English, who called it draughts (*drawtz*). In America it became known as checkers because it was played on a checkered board.

BILLIARDS

What we sometimes call "pool" started in northern Europe about 800 years ago. It was called ground billiards and was a lot like croquet—the game where you hit a ball through a little hoop in the grass with a wooden mallet. People didn't want to stop playing just because it was winter, so they moved the game inside and put it on a table. They chose the color green for the tops of their tables because it reminded them of grass.

MANCALA & WARI

One of the oldest games in the world, this counting and math game was first played in **Africa.** It could be played with shells, beads, pebbles, or seeds. Africans in the Americas could still play since they didn't need a game board or special pieces, just a quick mind.

DOMINOS

This is another **Chinese** game. The first tiles were made from animal bones with black ebony wood dots. The game traveled to Italy with the silk traders, and the tiles became black with white dots. The French named the game after the black and white hooded robe worn by priests at the time, which is called a *domino*. The name stuck!

DICE

In the ancient kingdom of **Mesopotamia** (*Mess-uh-po-TAME-ee-uh*), in what is now **Iraq**, folks loved board games. Dice were invented to tell people how many spaces to move their playing pieces. The Egyptians made dice from the heel bones of hoofed animals, and during the Middle Ages folks "rolled the bones" to predict the future.

IT'S RECESS

Jump rope and hopscotch have been around for thousands of years. Hopscotch was actually a way the ancient **Romans** trained their soldiers to improve their footwork, but a Roman soldier's hopscotch court was as long as a football field! Children watched the soldiers practice and began to imitate them.

Jumping rope was once something that grown men did in parts of the **Middle East** near the sea. Rope-makers made rope for sailing ships by twisting very long strands of hemp. As other workers brought the spinners more hemp, they had to jump over the twisting ropes. It was very dangerous!

Louis Armstrong was a jazz legend.

RED, WHITE, & THE BLUES

★

Long before there were *iPods*, there were people working in the sun, singing to make the long days pass more quickly. Music brought hope and joy.

Duke Ellington was a superstar in Jazz's heyday

SPIRITUALS & GOSPEL MUSIC

In the 1600s and 1700s, life was so hard for the enslaved Africans. They had no freedom, but there was one thing no one could take away from them—music! Music helped pass time as they worked. It was also a way to "talk" to other slaves without the master knowing. A new "music" began to take shape based on African rhythms. Words were added from folk tales and Bible stories and set to clapped, tapped beats. New instruments appeared too, such as the banjo, which is based on the African *ngoni* (*un-GO-nee*).

THE BLUES

A little slow, a little sad, the "Blues" was born as enslaved work crews built dams and roads along the Mississippi River. After the Civil War, these sad songs mixed together with the songs of the fields. A musician

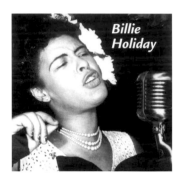

Billie Holiday

would sing a line, and the banjo would "answer" back with the same melody and beat. By the 1890s, the blues had spread across the country. Women were good at singing the blues too. At least when it came to music, we were all equal.

ALL THAT JAZZ

European music was all about the melody. African music was all about the beat. African Americans began to play "call-and-answer" music, making up their melodies "on-the-go" rather than following note-for-note compositions like Europe's musicians did. This new music—a combo of European and African sounds—grew into jazz. World War I (1914-1918) brought African Americans and their music to Europe, where jazz became a big hit. People there loved this exciting new music. By the 1920s jazz was being played everywhere! Africans in America had given the world a brand-new sound.

But there was still more music to be made...

FROM BLUEGRASS TO ROCK TO RAPPING

America's music is a quilt of different traditions. Take bluegrass—a mix of the traditional music of immigrants from the **British Isles** who settled in Appalachia stirred up with the sounds of rural African Americans. Country music also grew from British, Scot, and Irish folk roots.

Today rock music is the most popular music on the planet—a blend of African drum beats and strummed strings mixed with Europe's melodies. Rap is music's newest sound, but its roots go back to the *griots* (singer/storytellers) of **West Africa**. For centuries griots shared legends with spoken words and music. In the 1960s on the island of **Jamaica**, disc jockeys started rhyming as they cued up the next records at parties. As Jamaicans moved to America, that fun style came, too, and grew into rap music!

DANCE PARTY

You can't have music without dancing. Here are a few cool dance moves to bust!

SQUARE & LINE DANCING

As people from many lands began to settle in small towns, one of the things they did to relax was dance. But they came from different places with different dances, such as the polka from **Poland** or clog dancing from places such as **Ireland** and **Germany**. They shared their favorite steps with each other and got someone with a good memory to be a caller to remind folks what step to do next!

SALSA

Salsa is a spicy dip for chips, but it's also a hot and spicy style of dance. It got its start in New York City when folks from **Puerto Rico** added extra horns to a mix of **Afro-Cuban** beats. Other Latino dances include the *mambo* and *cha-cha*, which have fast little steps and lots of hip-shaking. *Reggaeton* is a new dance blend which mixes **Jamaican** dance music with Latin beats.

BREAK DANCING, HIP HOP, & FUNK

Today's dancers groove to a wide world of moves. We have borrowed from Asian Kung Fu and the **Afro-Brazilian** fighting art called *Capoeira (cah-PWEH-ra)*. We use the spins and dips of Europe's ballets, the arm movements of Hawaii's hula dancers, the hip shaking of salsa, and the quick-step footwork of both Native America's and Africa's dances to express ourselves!

WHAT MAKES US AMERICAN

Even though our neighbors may have different ethnic and cultural origins, we are still united as Americans by common ideas, traditions, and our acceptance of diversity in our communities.

TAKING PRIDE IN OUR ROOTS

We may call ourselves Americans, but we are all still proud of the places from which our families came. We enjoy celebrating with parties and parades that honor our heritage, and we wear our "roots" proudly!

WORKING TOGETHER

The people in this medical team come from very different backgrounds, but when it is time to go to work, none of that matters. They become a tight-knit, hardworking group devoted to keeping the people in their communities safe and healthy.

BECOMING AN AMERICAN CITIZEN

A **citizen** (SIT-uh-zin) is someone who, by birth or choice, is a member of a country. If you were born in the U.S.A, you are an American citizen, no matter where your parents were born. Being an American citizen means that you are protected by all of the laws of the United States and can vote when you are eighteen.

GETTING A TASTE OF OTHER CULTURES

What's for dinner tonight? Will it be Chinese, Italian, Mexican, Japanese, or Indian? How about Cajun, Cuban, French, or Middle Eastern? We love to sample new foods, which often become all-American favorites. What is your favorite?

TRYING NEW THINGS

Can a kid from Puerto Rico be a Tae Kwon Do champ? Can a child from Korea be an all-star cheerleader? Can a Filipino be a rock star? Here in America we get to choose from a whole wide world of activities, from Irish step-dancing to Japanese karate and more!

CELEBRATING AMERICA'S PAST

From Thanksgiving to Independence Day, everyone loves to gather together for all-American holidays. On Veterans Day and Memorial Day, flags fly, and we march proudly in parades. No matter where we were born, each of these days becomes a holiday for us all.

HOW DOES IT HAPPEN?

If people are not born in America but want to become U.S. citizens, they must do these things:

• *Live in America for at least five years.*
• *Be able to read, write, and speak English.*
• *Prove that they are good, honest people.*
• *Know all about our government.*
• *Pass a written test of American history.*

Many people who take the test end up knowing more about America than people who have been born here!

UNITED BY LAW

One of the most important links among all Americans is a special group of laws—the *Constitution*—a document that unites and protects us as a single group of people even though we come from many different backgrounds. No matter what language we speak in our homes, no matter what holidays we celebrate, America has grown strong because we have learned to share and to lend a hand to both our fellow Americans and the citizens of the world when they need help.

AMERICAN STORIES

Some people leave lasting marks on the world. They teach us that being strong, brave, and hard-working has nothing to do with the color of our hair, eyes, or skin.

Some of these people moved to America from other lands. Some were born here. Each has done something special.

Biographies are books about famous people. The library has many from which to choose. By reading them we can learn how to be great ourselves!

Ask your librarian for books about these great women and men.

BREAKING DOWN WALLS

1913-2005

Rosa Parks was a seamstress. One night in 1955, on the long bus ride home, she broke the law by not giving her seat to a white man. That small action for equal rights helped start the **civil rights** movement.

1919-1972

Jackie Robinson was one of the greatest baseball players ever. Before him, men of color were not allowed to play major league baseball. Jackie was spat on, ignored, and booed, but in time his grace and skill won him many fans.

Susan B. Anthony faced a different kind of discrimination. Her skin was not dark. She did not come from far away, but she was a *woman* and in her day, women did not have equal rights. They couldn't vote. She fought to change that.
1820-1906

FIGHTING FOR FAIRNESS

1829-1909

Geronimo was an Apache leader who tried to keep his nation's lands from being taken by the U.S. government. His real name was Goyathlay, and he became world-famous as a symbol of bravery.

1880-1968

Helen Keller became very ill when she was a baby. When she recovered, she could no longer hear or see. In spite of these handicaps she became a champion for equal rights for the disabled.

1835-1919

Andrew Carnegie came to America from Scotland at the age of thirteen and worked his way up from a factory boy to a steel tycoon. He made a huge fortune and built more than 2,500 public libraries.

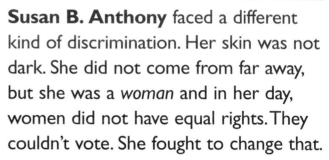

MAKING LIFE NICER

1917-

I.M. Pei came from China when he was eighteen to learn how to design buildings. He went on to become one of the world's most famous architects by creating all sorts of amazing structures.

1888-1989

Irving Berlin was born in Russia and came here when he was five. He ran away from home and sang for spare change. He wrote over 1,500 songs—some of the most famous ever—such as *God Bless America, White Christmas,* and *Easter Parade.*

1954-

Oprah Winfrey had a tough childhood, but she turned her life around. At the age of seventeen, she began working for a local radio station. Today she is a legend and one of the best known people in the world.

CARING AND SHARING

1821-1912

Clara Barton was a nurse during the Civil War. She started the American Red Cross so that people could pitch in to help wounded soldiers, whether they fought for the North or the South.

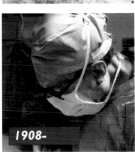
1908-

Michael DeBakey, a Lebanese American, became one of the world's most famous doctors and heart surgeons. He also created Mobile Army Surgical Hospital (M.A.S.H.) units, which saved thousands of soldiers' lives in wartime.

1936-1990

Jim Henson was the wonderful Muppet-maker who taught us that green frogs, pink pigs, big yellow birds, grubby green grouches, and blue monsters could all be best friends. If *they* can be friends, so can we all!

AMAZING PEOPLE

There are many people who have made America great whose names you might not know. Here are just a few.

Luis Alvares–This Nobel Prize winning Hispanic-American scientist helped develop radar and more.

Benito Flores–This Filipino electrician took a discovery by a brilliant Serbian-American inventor named **Nicola Tesla,** and built a simple <u>florescent</u> light bulb. He got to name it after himself!

Enrico Fermi—He left Italy to save his family during World War II and played a big part in figuring out how to create atomic energy.

Sequoyah—A Cherokee, he was one of the only people in history to create an entire alphabet and grammar for a language. Giant Sequoia trees and Sequoia National Park were named after him.

c.1766–1843

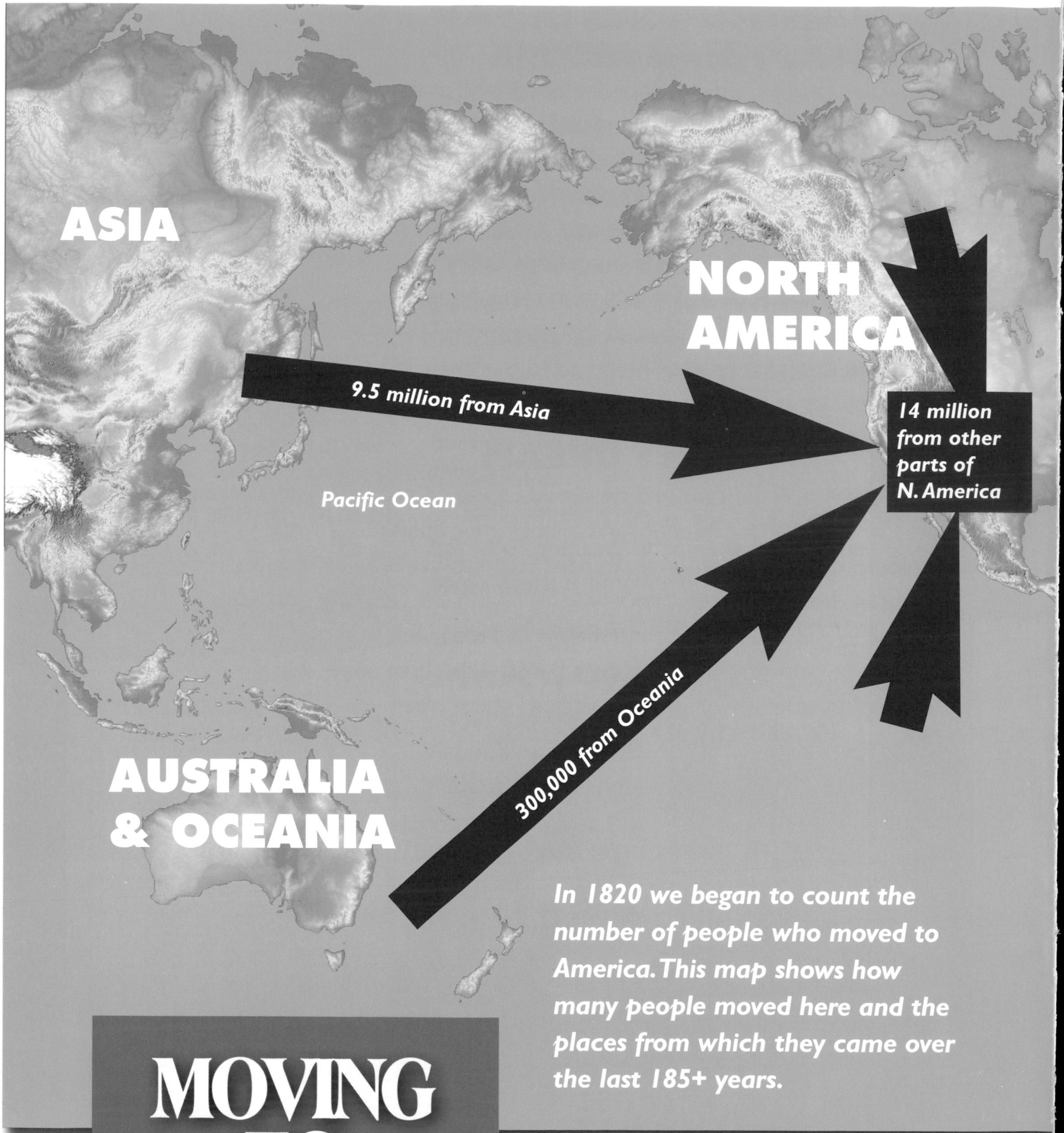

ASIA

NORTH
AMERICA

9.5 million from Asia

14 million
from other
parts of
N. America

Pacific Ocean

AUSTRALIA
& OCEANIA

300,000 from Oceania

In 1820 we began to count the
number of people who moved to
America. This map shows how
many people moved here and the
places from which they came over
the last 185+ years.

MOVING TO AMERICA

ON THE MOVE

Every year, a million more people move
to the United States. One hundred years
ago most immigrants came from
Europe. Today that has changed.

EUROPE

39 million from Europe

About 1 million from Africa*

3.5 million from South America

Atlantic Ocean

AFRICA

SOUTH
AMERICA

* Between 1500 and 1820 about 10 million Africans were seized as slaves and brought to both North and South America. About half a million were taken directly to the U. S. More recently, many people from Africa have begun to move to America because they _want_ to—finding good jobs and a chance for new beginnings.

THE U.S.A. TODAY

In the last twenty years most people have come to the United States from Asia, Latin America, the Caribbean, and Africa. They are changing our culture in a whole new way.

As people from all over the world live side by side—working, learning, and playing—the labels that identify us—Irish-American or Filipino-American or African American—may slowly begin to vanish.

INDEX

Give me your tired, your poor,

Your huddled masses yearning to breathe free,

The wretched refuse of your teeming shore,

Send these, the homeless, tempest-tossed to me,

I lift my lamp beside the golden door!

From The New Colossus,
a poem by Emma Lazarus,
inscribed at the base of
the Statue of Liberty